THE CRY OF THE SOUL

THE CRY OF THE SOUL
MYSTIC POETRY

by
Darshan Singh

SAWAN KIRPAL PUBLICATIONS

This is number

76

of
the limited Case-bound Edition
of 500 Copies
published on
6th February 1977

Library of Congress Catalog: 77-72197
ISBN Number: 0-918224-02-0
ISBN Number: 0-918224-03-9 (Hardcover)

Printed in the United States of America

First Edition: February 6, 1977

Sawan Kirpal Publications

Hazur Baba Sawan Singh Ji Maharaj
(1858-1948)

Param Sant Kirpal Singh Ji Maharaj
(1894-1974)

These
flowers of devotion
are offered
at
the Lotus Feet
of
Hazur Baba Sawan Singh Ji Maharaj
under Whose spiritual guidance eternal lamps have
been lit in the dark path of my life,
and in the light of which I am treading toward the
goal of universal brotherhood and love,

and
to
Param Sant Kirpal Singh Ji Maharaj,
my revered Father,
Who brought up this insignificant creature in
His spiritual lap, and Who molded my life
according to
the highest spiritual values.

TABLE OF CONTENTS

Introduction	13
Resplendent Glorious Master	23
Word Made Flesh	25
To the Loved One	27
Prayer to the Beloved of Spring	29
Anguished Outburst of the Forlorn	30
Revelations	32
A Prayer	33
The Blessed Day	35
Adieu O Beloved of the Universe	36
Greetings to Our Brothers and Sisters in God	37
A Tear from the Master's Eye	38
On the August Return of the Universal Cup-Bearer	39
An Ode	41
In Memory of Baba Sawan Singh	45
Sant Samagam	47
The Cry of the Soul	49
Master of Light and Life	52
Felicitations	56
Champion of the Caravan of Love	59

The Elixir of Love	61
In Memoriam	63
The Embodiment of Love Divine	66
Advent of the Universal Cup-Bearer	70
Elegy on the Passing Away of the Beloved Master	72

Living Master Sant Darshan Singh Ji Maharaj

INTRODUCTION

I

THE POEMS

Sant Darshan Singh's Urdu poems are written in a classic and highly stylized form in the Persian tradition. In India he is acclaimed as a master of this form. He began writing poetry at the age of seventeen, and his poems, which all have an underlying spiritual theme, cover a wide variety of subjects.

With the exception of "Greetings to Our Brothers and Sisters in God" and "A Tear from the Master's Eye," which were both written in English, all the poems in this collection have been translated from Urdu by the poet himself. They represent only a handful from the large body of poetry he has composed. Nearly all the pieces selected for this collection have been inspired by the poet's devoted love for his own great spiritual Master, Hazur Baba Sawan Singh Ji of Beas, and for Sant Kirpal Singh Ji who was Baba Sawan Singh Ji's spiritual successor and the poet's Father.

Sant Darshan Singh has already published two collections of poems: *Talash-e-Noor* (*Quest for Light*) and *Manzil-e-Noor* (*Abode of Light*). Both of these books were publicly acclaimed, and they established the author as the leading Urdu mystic poet of his generation. He, however, attributes his success not to himself. As he puts it:

> Because the Beloved Master, Sant Kirpal Singh Ji, went through all my poems and corrected them wherever necessary, it has

been my good fortune that they carry the gift of His charging. So if my poetry has caught the public eye and moved the heart of the reader, the credit for this goes entirely to my Beloved Father and my spiritual mentor, Hazur Baba Sawan Singh Ji Maharaj. They have been bestowing these revelations, and I have only been carrying out the stenographic work.

According to Sant Darshan Singh, "Poetry is a vehicle for the expression of one's innermost thoughts, and as such my poetry has a mystic dimension." He further says, "Mysticism is the only way to evolve cosmos out of chaos."

This collection of Sant Darshan Singh's poems range over a period of thirty-six years. He tells us, however, that in translations of Urdu poetry, generally not only is the form lost, but also the rhythm and resonance, and that even the meaning may become obscure if the symbolism is not understood. In Persian mystic poetry the spiritual Master is often referred to as the Beloved, the Cup-Bearer, or the Lord of the Tavern; very often—as in the mystic poetry of the Christian Saint John of the Cross—these poems read like love lyrics. Indeed, the *Rubaiyat* of Omar Khayyam, contrary to popular belief, have a spiritual not a sensual meaning. Such poets describe God-intoxication as the wine freely poured out by the Master to His devotees.

Symbolism is the highest form of Urdu and Persian poetry, and the emphasis is not only on the structure of the verses, but also on the compression of a whole world of meaning into a single verse as in the form known as the *ghazal* or lyric. This symbolism can often be interpreted on different levels — that of physical love and of mystic love.

Most of the poems in this collection sing of the relationship of the devotee to his spiritual Master, the Beloved. The Beloved is a God-realized soul, and the devotee passionately desires to become one with Him. Sant Darshan Singh's poems burn with the anguished intensity of that desire; the soul can know no rest until it is one with the Beloved, joined in mystic marriage. When this happens, the devotee then becomes one with the Master, and through His unbounded Grace, attains union with God, which is the real purpose of human life.

Masters of all religions have given out the same message: as men we are all one in spite of outer differences, we are all children of the same God, and the purpose of human life is the conscious union of the soul with God. This can be achieved by the Grace of a Godman Who, at the time of Initiation, links the soul with the inner Light and inner Sound, which are the two primal manifestations of God vibrating through His whole Creation. Thus the soul starts on its journey back Home ever under the guidance and protection of the Master. The Masters teach that we must live a life of universal brotherhood and non-injury to any living creature. If we accept this, a vegetarian diet becomes imperative. The Masters also emphasize the essential unity of all religions and They advocate a chaste life, selfless service, and love for all. Indeed, the whole impetus and inspiration of this spiritual Path rests on love. It has been called the Path of Love—love above all for the Guru Whose benign and bliss-giving Presence reawakens the dormant spirit in us. However, this is also a Path of anguish and tears as many of Sant Darshan Singh's poems bear out, for this burning love can know no rest until the soul becomes one with the Beloved. As he himself puts it:

> Poetry is in reality the cry of the soul, and it usually expresses pangs of separation. Poems are born not out of intoxication produced by wine, but from passion and anguish flowing spontaneously from the heart.

Sant Darshan Singh's poems vividly shine for us with the poet's passionate devotion to his Beloved; they sing to us with his God-intoxication; they pierce us with the anguish and ecstasy of the spiritual Path; but above all, they fire us with divine longing to reach the same Goal and fill us with the perseverance and inspiration necessary to tread the journey Home.

II
THE POET

Darshan Singh was born on 14th September 1921 at Kountrilla, a village in the Rawalpindi District which is now part of Pakistan. His father, Sant Kirpal Singh Ji (1894-1974), had been a spiritual seeker from an early age, and in 1924 was to find the answer to his searchings when he met Hazur Baba Sawan Singh Ji (1858-1948) at Beas in the Punjab. From then on the Beas Saint became the guiding light for the entire family. Darshan was barely six when Baba Sawan Singh Ji initiated him into the mystery of the Word—the Surat Shabd Yoga or the Yoga of the Sound Current. Reborn of the spirit, the child ran straight to his father, exclaiming, "Father, father, how far have you got initiation? I have been initiated up to the stars!"

It was Hazur Himself Who was later to lay the foundation of Darshan's literary career by directing him to take up Persian and History in College rather than the physical sciences to which the young man was then inclined. This led to an infatuation with Persian and Urdu mystic poetry which grew over the years and has inspired him to use that form for his own verses.

When Darshan was seventeen years old he composed his first poem in honor of his Beloved Hazur. His father wrote out a hemistich—the first half of the opening verse—and then asked Darshan to complete the poem; it was recited at Hazur's next birthday celebration at Beas and was received with much acclaim. The Gracious Hazur asked Darshan to repeat several verses—a gesture which in India is the highest form of appreciation. This poem makes a fitting opening to the present collection.

Two years after this auspicious debut, Darshan Singh presided over a Poetry Symposium at Beas held in honor of Hazur's birthday. From then on he was to recite many of his poems at important Satsangs, and in course of time he also became a distinguished figure in Urdu literary circles. Sant Kirpal Singh Ji had written many poems in honor of Hazur both in Urdu and Punjabi under the pen name of "Jamal." His son was to carry on the same tradition, and writes his verses under the *nom de plume* of "Darshan."

In 1965 Darshan Singh published his first collection of poems, *Talash-e-Noor* (*Quest for Light*); Sant Kirpal Singh Ji wrote the Foreword, and in it He drew attention to the universal message of all the great prophets and saints of the East and West in whose honor these poems were written. Krishna, Buddha, Mahavira, Zoroaster, Christ, Mohammed and Nanak are some of the divine Godmen whom the poet has bound together in his outpourings of love.

This book was followed in 1969 by a second collection, *Manzil-e-Noor* (*Abode of Light*). It was written for the quincentenary of Guru Nanak's birth, and pays homage to the life and teachings of this great Apostle of Peace. This volume won for the poet the Urdu Academy Award, and established Darshan Singh as the most distinguished living mystic poet writing in Urdu.

Sant Darshan Singh firmly believes that to solve

any problem we have to go to the root, and his poetry repeatedly directs us to the Spirit and to the life of the Spirit as the source of everything. He regards poetry primarily as a divine gift which enables man to express his innermost spiritual longings, and he believes that mystic poetry is born out of the desire to attain spiritual heights through self-discipline and the controlling of worldly desires. The Masters of the Surat Shabd Yoga do not believe in negative mysticism—renouncing the world and retiring to the jungle; They teach positive mysticism, an inner detachment which enables one to face the duties and problems of every-day life while living in the world. They live by the general pattern of Their respective societies; They always earn Their own living, and never live on the offerings of Their devotees.

In this tradition, Darshan Singh on reaching twenty-one entered Government Service in Delhi, and over the years has risen to the position of a Deputy Secretary to the Government of India. In 1943, a year after he began his career, he married; he has two sons, and lives in Delhi. While living in the world and fulfilling his worldly obligations, he has pursued his spiritual quest, and his poetry is a living testimony to the intensity of that quest.

A great turning point occurred in 1948 which changed Darshan Singh's whole life: Hazur Baba Sawan Singh Ji Maharaj left this earth plane during His ninety-first year, and the spiritual mantle fell on the poet's father, Sant Kirpal Singh Ji, Who then became the Living Master of the Surat Shabd Yoga. Darshan Singh then began to serve his father as the Universal Father just as he had served his Beloved Hazur. His poetry took on a new impetus: the Master Power never dies, and Darshan Singh's verses sang forth to honor the new human pole in which It was now manifest. These rich outpourings continued throughout the following twenty-six years of his Father's Ministry, and many outstanding examples have been included in this collection.

When Sant Kirpal Singh Ji was nearing the end of His spiritual work on this earth plane He passed on His spiritual Power through the eyes to Darshan Singh on the night of 19th August 1974, as His own Satguru had passed It on to Him twenty-six years earlier. Since then Sant Darshan Singh has been carrying the Torch of Spirituality as the Living Master of the Surat Shabd Yoga, and is bestowing the sacred gift of Holy Naam Initiation to seekers after Truth all over the world.

Kate Tillis
21st November 1976
Rajpur, India

Sant Darshan Singh reciting his poetry in the presence of Sant Kirpal Singh Ji Maharaj.

Sant Darshan Singh reciting his poetry in the presence of Hazur Baba Sawan Singh Ji Maharaj at Beas.

RESPLENDENT GLORIOUS MASTER

This poem was written in 1938 when Darshan Singh was just seventeen years old; it was his first poem in honor of Hazur Baba Sawan Singh Ji Maharaj.

The Light of God has manifested itself in the form of the Resplendent Glorious Master. He is the mirror which reflects the Eternal Creator.

What a wonder! God speaks through the human form. How strange! Even then He moves about unperceived unless He initiates mortals into the Mysteries of the Universe beyond.

O Beauty embodied and Grace personified, whosoever casts a glance at Thy radiant form becomes self-oblivious and lost in trance. He would fain lay himself as a sacrifice at Thy Holy Feet.

Thy fame has spread over hills and dales, oceans and continents, this transitory world and the world beyond. All lips sing of Thy benevolence, every heart bears the seal of Thy Universal Love.

O seekers of communion with the Creator, come behold the Universal Master because He has consciously merged Himself in God and become one with Him.

The glory and grace of my Master manifest themselves in every direction. My heart is inebriate with His Love. I see His effulgent smiling face in every atom.

It is our short-sightedness to think that the sphere over which His tresses† sway is limited. In fact the sphere which His tresses engulf and enliven is unlimited.

Word has been made flesh and dwells amongst us. Although His glimpses can often be seen in this ephemeral world, yet in reality that Paragon of Beauty is always enthroned in the highest heavenly abode.

If the unseen God be the Captain of the ship of life, let Him be. What have I to do with Him? The Captain of my ship of life is my Beloved Master Sawan. This is sufficient for me.

O Nectar of Immortality, how can a mortal do justice to Thy glory? Thou art the solver of all problems. Thou art the liberator of mankind from the cycle of births and deaths. O perennial source of bliss, Thou hast brought us in touch with the revitalizing Word—the Sound Current—which rings through eternity, upholds the Universe and vibrates in every heart.

I need only a life-inspiring glance of Thine, O Beloved! Thy divine touch is a panacea for all my sorrows and afflictions.

I pray to Thee, O Universal Cup-Bearer, to bestow a draught of Thy divine vintage on destitute Darshan, lying prostrate at Thy threshold.

---

† *In mysticism, tresses is a symbol for spiritual influence.*

WORD MADE FLESH

This poem was written to celebrate Baba Sawan Singh Ji's birthday on 27th July 1940.

O Sawan Lord! God in man
So bounteous, kind and gay,
Thou established the kingdom of God on earth
To anguish of souls allay.

When Thou assumed the human form
Thou found a bewildered world—
Men and women had wrecked themselves
In Mammon's cockpit hurled.

"Like snow-white swan and lily pure,
Pass thy life" Thou sayeth,
"Although thou livest in a pool of mire,
In air dry wings do spread."

"Know thyself and then thy God,
Respond to the spiritual call.
Resign to thy Master's Will
All thy actions, great or small.

"Talk not of fate but lean on Him
For He can improve thy fate.
In Him thy love and faith combine,
He'll open the Heavenly Gate."

White beard, hoary head, clothes snowy white,
Thy figure's a heavenly dream.
No need to yearn for the unseen God,
We behold the Father Supreme.

In grief and sorrow to Thee we come
Forlorn, sinful and weak.
No friend but Thee we have on earth,
Thy Heavenly help we seek.

Were every hair of mine a tongue,
It's hard to sing Thy praise.
Words can't do justice to Thy theme,
No language can express Thy ways.

O Sawan Lord! Make me, Thy slave,
A flute in Thy hands to play.
Let the Elixir of Thy Holy Breath
Flow through my frame of clay.

On the holy occasion of Thy birthday,
At Thy threshold we pray;
Bestow on us Thy bounteous Grace
And wash our sins away.

TO THE LOVED ONE

This poem was written shortly after Baba Sawan Singh Ji left the earth-plane in 1948.

Pour forth the wine from Thy intoxicating
 eyes, O Love,

And with the vision of Thy beauty, make
 us mad, O Love.

Tell us the secret of life that we be
 lost to worldly woes, O Love.

If heart and soul be the price, cease not
 but pour, for we shall pay with all, O Love.

Our yearning for Thee has made us
 impatient, O Love.

O! Lift the veil from within that we
 may behold Thee, O Love.

Look at the overcast sky unburdening
 itself, O Love.

Spill forth Thy wine in like
 measure, O Love.

And let the wine of oneness so
 overwhelm us, O Love,

That all distinctions and divisions
 be lost, O Love.

Thy divine vintage has at last
 cleansed me, O Love.

Now unfold the mystery
  of the two worlds, O Love.

May Thy tavern be ever
  filled, O Love!

And may the wine of Thy lotus eyes
  ever flow freely, O Love!

We implore Thee in the name of Thine
  intoxicating eyes, O Love,

Let us drink this day without
  any measure, O Love.

Thy "Darshan" has come for Thy
  darshan (glimpse), O Love.

Grant him the wine of Thy
  vision, O Love.

PRAYER TO THE BELOVED OF SPRING

This poem was written in the early 1950's in memory of Baba Sawan Singh Ji.

What does it matter if flowers have blossomed, when our drooping hearts have not blossomed this spring? Let fire be struck to this spring if You be not here.

I am that spring-nourished bud which was unfortunately robbed of the charms of blossoming. The Nourishing Deity bade farewell to this earthly sojourn just when I was going to savour the quintessence of spring.

Such a devastating autumn has swept over the orchard of my heart that there appears no hope of the blossoming spring ever returning and rejuvenating it.

Alas! the elegance, hue and briskness of the assembly of lovers were plundered in the very prime of spring. Woe betide me! Heartrending melodies are bursting forth from the strings of their broken hearts.

O tender-hearted Beloved of Spring! Are You not moved by lamentations of these love-lorn hearts? We pray You in the name of Eternal Love to grace and bless us with Your life-inspiring radiant glimpses, and blossom our drooping hearts again this spring.

ANGUISHED OUTBURST OF THE FORLORN

This was written in pangs of separation from Baba Sawan Singh Ji in the 1950's.

The tavern is deserted. The goblet and the cup are in sad plight. Alas! With Your departure the blossoming spring has turned its face on our thirsty souls.

Years have crawled by—nay, it seems that ages have passed since Your resplendent face, Your beautiful flowing white beard and Your ecstasy-producing eyes were hidden from our physical sight. This tavern, every atom of which was charged with Your life-inspiring glances and which was an object of envy even for paradise, is now a God-forsaken place. The intoxicated assembly of Your devotees has been robbed of their bliss and tranquility. Alas! Autumn has completely swayed over their blossoming and spring-nourished lives. Their life without You cannot be termed as "life" in the true sense of the word. It is in reality a continuous torture.

It is true that even now You are protecting and guiding us. The lucky ones, who traverse beyond the physical plane, do converse with You at will. But even then, so long as we assume physical bodies, Your physical form had its own charm for us. Had it not been so, the greatest Saints of all times would not have pined and longed for the physical sight of their Masters in addition to the inner radiant Light. Their long vigils, their incessant tears, their spontaneous outpourings and pangs of separation, so exquisitely portrayed in some of their revelations, bear ample testimony to this point.

Every moment of separation is like dissolution to us. We are restlessly waiting for the elevating sight of our Cup-Bearer—that Cup-Bearer with whose bewitching eyes even the angels would fall in love. If He were to raise His enthralling eyes, even nature would become inebriated. Our restless souls are lamenting in separation, and praying at the Lotus Feet of the Universal Cup-Bearer. He is the very soul of spirituality, the Light of God—nay, He is God personified! He assumed the human garb of Sawan to quench the spiritual thirst of millions.

REVELATIONS

This poem was written in praise of Hazur in the 1950's.

You have set afloat the perennial fountains of eternal bliss and everlasting ecstasy. You have brought forth fragrant roses where there were pricking thorns before.

You have removed all differences between the theists and the atheists. You have brought together Christians and pagans through the Music of the Spheres.

You have taught us the divine language which is both unspoken and unwritten. You have solved for us the mystery of life and death.

By setting an example of ideal and simple life, You have lifted the veils of illusion from the face of the earth.

Your intoxicated eyes are overflowing cups of divine wine. You have set aplunder the treasures of spirituality through Your enlivening glances.

It is our good fortune that in this ephemeral existence You have initiated us into the mysteries of eternal life.

It is the wonder of Your everlasting Grace, O Master Divine, that You have brought about communion between man and his Creator.

A PRAYER

This was written in the 1950's in sweet remembrance of Baba Sawan Singh Ji.

O Eternal Cup-Bearer, for God's sake take care of Your forlorn thirsty souls who are pining for Your Divine wine! Kindly put them in trance again through Your ecstasy-producing glances.

Why have You concealed Your resplendent face from our physical sight? How long will this indifference continue? O Universal Cup-Bearer, for Heaven's sake lift the veil from Your radiant face.

If my heart, my soul, this world and the hereafter are a price of Your eternal love, I would fain sacrifice all these at Your altar. Accept them, O Beloved, not as a price for Your Grace but only as a humble token for Thy manifold blessings.

The ambrosia laden dark clouds have overcast the sky. We implore You to favor us likewise with Your boundless life-inspiring eternal wine, so that we may drink to our hearts' content.

Your eyes are overflowing with inebriating wine. Your elevating glances carry one on the Path of Love leading to the ultimate communion of soul with the Oversoul.

Kindly make me quite oblivious of this material world and its affairs through Your rapturous glances, and then reveal the secrets of both the worlds to me.

May Your tavern be an abode of eternal bliss and tranquility! Kindly pour out pitchers of wine from Your narcissus eyes.

O glorious Cup-Bearer, we beseech You in the name of Your own Beloved Master to bestow on Your pining devotees as much wine as they can drink.

THE BLESSED DAY
(6th February, 1894)

This poem was written in celebration of Sant Kirpal Singh Ji's birthday in 1955, and was published later that year in one of the first editions of the Urdu Sat Sandesh.

Blessed was the day when the Eternal Light manifested itself in this transitory world in the form of the Glorious Resplendent Master.

Blessed was the day when all the beauty and grace of the heavens condensed themselves in the form of the Beloved of the Universe.

Blessed was the day when the ambrosia-laden clouds of Divine Grace poured forth showers on this parched earth.

Blessed was the day when on the arrival of the Universal Cup-Bearer, the goblet was in ecstasy and the cup fell in trance.

With the advent of Kirpal, the tavern of God overflowed with the vintage divine.

He is the Universal Cup-Bearer, He is the Nectar of Immortality, He is the Light of God.

It is through His Grace alone that the human heart manifests the Eternal Light and the Holy Harmony.

ADIEU O BELOVED OF THE UNIVERSE

This was written on the departure of Sant Kirpal Singh Ji for His first World Tour in May, 1955, and recited at Sawan Ashram, Delhi.

You are that everlasting bliss, that eternal wine, that divine ecstasy which brings about communion between man and his Creator.

You are that magic-producing glance, that life-inspiring eye, that ennobling touch which converts mortals into immortals.

You belong to the East as well as the West, You belong to the North as well as the South— nay, You belong neither to the East nor to the West, neither to the North nor to the South alone. You are the Universal Cup-Bearer and the whole world is Your tavern.

Adieu! O Lord of the Universe. Go and convey Your deathless Message to every living soul on the face of this transitory world. But for Sawan's sake do not forget that You belong to us as well.

GREETINGS TO OUR BROTHERS AND SISTERS IN GOD

This poem was written the day after the preceding one, and sent to Mr. T. S. Khanna who printed it and circulated it in the West.

Felicitations, O brothers and sisters in God!
The Universal Cup-Bearer comes to you
Holding His goblet of the Elixir of Life
To bestow on you His everlasting bounty.

His hands, God's hands; His eyes, God's eyes;
His words, life-inspiring; His touch, so sublime.
He is Grace embodied; He is Love personified;
He is the fountainhead of bliss, eternal and divine.

Behold the Living God treading this earth,
He'll open the Heavenly Gate to you.
He'll take you beyond the physical plane
To have communion with the Almighty.

We, your fellow-seekers for Water of Life,
Pray to the Divine Master Kirpal,
To infuse you with Spirit immortal,
And bless you with life eternal.

A TEAR FROM THE MASTER'S EYE

When the Beloved Master was on His first World Tour in 1955, He received many heartrending letters from His devotees left behind in India who were feeling the pangs of separation. Sant Darshan learned that on reading such letters tears were seen in the eyes of the Beloved Master. He explains that he wrote the following poem when he visualized one such tear — one only, for he could not bear the thought of any more.

**This quivering glistening tear on Your eyelashes
Appears to be a shining star detached from the vault of the bedecked azure sky
Or pure mercury sparkling when full of warmth
Or a lustrous pearl coming out of an oyster
Or a charm-casting spell for all onlookers
Or a transparent dew drop on the blooming rose at dawn
Or a glittering atom glorified by the rays of the sun.
Nay—it has no parallel. In reality the Eternal Cup-Bearer's bowl is overflowing.
It symbolizes the eternal story of Divine Love and Grace.
The loving memory of the dear ones
Draws life from every vein into flowing eyes
Where it is transformed into a tear through the alchemy of love.
This tear—this wonderful tear—points out the way for ultimate communion of man with his Creator.**

ON THE AUGUST RETURN OF THE UNIVERSAL CUP-BEARER

On the Beloved Master's return to India in November, 1955, after His first World Tour, this poem of welcome was recited at Sawan Ashram, Delhi.

The atmosphere is dancing in jubilation, the cup is in trance: Somebody has returned with the message of Spring.

Which ecstasy-producing inebriated Cup-Bearer has set His foot in this assembly of drunkards today? He has again brought cup after cup of the Elixir of Life into continuous circulation.

The ambrosia-laden clouds of Divine Grace have overcast the sky. The Beloved of the Universe has come again on the edge of the roof waving His long tresses.

Your august presence has brought such an elevating atmosphere in the valley of Love that my soul is stealthily withdrawing from the body and concentrating at the third eye.

Whose intoxicating name has come on my lips this day that I have become tipsy and self-oblivious without the worldly wine and the earthly cup?

O seekers after Truth, I congratulate you from the core of my heart because after showering His everlasting bounties on the denizens of the West, the Universal Cup-Bearer has come to the East again.

It is a manifestation of His boundless Grace that the Bestower of Eternal Bliss has returned from the colorful and enticing continents of materialism to bless this simple land of spirituality.

In reality it is the wonder of the Eternal Cup-Bearer's narcissus-like eyes that the atmosphere is dancing and the cup is in trance.

AN ODE

This was recited on the occasion of the Investiture Ceremony held in Delhi on 2nd September 1962, at which the Order of St. John of Jerusalem, Knights of Malta, was conferred upon H.H. Sant Kirpal Singh Ji Maharaj.

A kindly heart offers a vintage of God-Knowledge,
    and infuses the breath of life in the clayey mold.

It awakens the spirit in the human body, and
    kindles therein the Light of God.

It delivers to man the message of love, and
    lights in him the torch of true knowledge.

It grants true wisdom to human understanding, and
    alchemizes an atom into a brilliant sun.

It fills dry bones with the light of life, and
    floods the arid soul with the waters divine.

Physical life is all misery, but
    peace comes as the spirit grows in strength.

The social orders are at discord, and
    the soul lies low under the dead weight of mind and matter.

The value of the body counts supreme everywhere,
    and religions have degenerated into delusion.

All men are after name and fame, and
    have forgotten the purpose of life.

Spiritual embellishment is the goal of life, and
    cosmic awakening is the real end.

He who understands the problem of life, grows into a Qalendar,† and in wisdom waxes like a sea.

Blessed indeed art Thou, the Beloved Master, for Thou hast understood the mystery of life.

Thy message is one of wisdom divine—a message of kindly love and affection.

Thy religion is one of selfless service to man, with an ideal of love for all.

The world peopled by diverse races can come to its own by affection alone.

Thou art filled with the holy light of divine wisdom, and maketh no distinction between man and man.

All distinctions of race and color are naught, all men are but men in Thy holy presence.

All creatures are from the one Creator, and He alone is the Cup-Bearer to the tipplers in His tavern.

The moment a soul contacts the saving life-lines, it becomes one with the eternal life principle.

---

† *Qalendar: A mystic, who gives up all worldly possessions and travels from place to place to deliver the Eternal Message of God to aspiring souls.*

All nations and nationalities are but blossoms—
   blossoms from the garden of the Most High.

Many may be the drinkers and each with a separate
   cup, yet the world is but one tavern craving the
   vintage divine.

Countries and cities make no difference, for
   all spring from the same source.

All religions teach of the one Truth—the Truth of
   universal peace, wisdom and love.

All preach of what is good and great, and
   each gives out Truth in its own way.

All faiths and creeds have but one message to give,
   for spiritual emancipation is the goal of each.

Ram and Rahim may seemingly appear as
   separate, but both are flowers on the one bough,
   and both smell sweet.

Mold your life in loving devotion, and
   follow the path of Nanak and Kabir.

From the flute of Krishna flows forth the music of
   love, and he who hears it gets lost in intoxication.

Do obeisance unto Mohammed, but
   forget not the teachings of Christ.

The son of man is Word personified, for
   He teaches love, light and life.

Love of God and man is His greatest message, and
   He talks and walks in the ways of God.

He scruples not to give out Truth, and
   for Truth He smilingly carries His own cross.

In different garbs appear the Lovers of the Lord—
   like flowers They appear in the holy soil of God.

O Master, Thy message is one for entire humanity—
   it is one of love and friendship alike for all.

The whole world dotes on Thee with loving
   adoration, and is proud of its darling son.

All men benefit from Thy august presence—
   even the mighty Himalayas owe their grandeur
   to Thee.

As the sun of spirituality rises in the horizon, Thy
   spiritual greatness grows from strength to
   strength.

How can the finite sing of the Infinite, for
   Thou art the accredited leader in divinity.

Thou art love personified and the true son of
   Sawan.

Thou art the radiant sun of spirituality, and
   Knighthood does Thee but little honor.

These are but flowers from the garden of love—
   O Beloved, accept them in Thy munificence
   sublime.

IN MEMORY OF BABA SAWAN SINGH

This poem was written in the 1960's.

Thy call hath brought to life the slumbering ages,
Thy song has gladdened the hearts of all;
All are dancing to the music of Thy soul—
Hail to Thee! O Lord of the tavern.

Thy Name gives comfort in all our woes,
For we all live by the life-breath of Thy giving;
Thou art a lode-star that leads us on and on—
Hail to Thee! O Lord of the tavern.

From the dust of Thy Feet springs the Light of Life,
The breath of Thy being enlivens one and all;
Thy smile turns autumn into fragrant spring—
Hail to Thee! O Lord of the tavern.

O Lord! the world is at enmity with peace and
 goodwill,
The structure of life is torn to shreds;
May Thou uplift the earth with Thy magic call
 of love—
Hail to Thee! O Lord of the tavern.

Thy greatness shines in the House of the Lord,
All Thy wonders we find in Thy Kirpal;
O wake us up to life in Thy living tavern—
Hail to Thee! O Lord of the tavern.

All the great sit in loving congregation at Thy Feet,
World-weary and tired they come seeking Thy aid;
For Thou alone art a Messiah for all their ills—
Hail to Thee! O Lord of the tavern.

From Thee we get the quintessence of all the
    Masters past;
At Thy door we see the world knit as one,
Friends and foes alike losing all their discord—
Hail to Thee! O Lord of the tavern.

O remove the veil that hides Thy face divine,
And let us drink the Water of Life from Thy dazzling
    glance;
For a glimpse of that glance of love, I roam the
    world over—
Hail to Thee! O Lord of the tavern.

SANT SAMAGAN

This poem was recited at the Gandhi Grounds, Delhi, on 9th February 1964, at a public reception for the Beloved Master who had just returned to India from His Second World Tour.

As the clouds of despair gather thick and fast, the
 world stands in dread of a fearful doom;
The peoples are sundered one from the other,
 groping for a way out of the dreadful gloom.
The flame of pseudo love with its lurid light is
 shedding tremulous shadows on the tangled
 sea of life.
In the deepening darkness there is not a ray of
 hope, and all stand helpless in their molds
 of flesh.

The centrifugal force of love spreads far and wide
 when pumped from the heart of holy souls,
And man comes nearer to man as the barriers fall —
 the barriers of race, religion and clan.
The Grand Family of Man stands one, all men
 shining like stars in a clear blue sky.
This is the alchemy of love, transmuting the baser
 elements into sterling gold.

Deeply buried in the human heart lies the kingly
 power of love, far from human ken,
And men move, mendicants in search of bliss
 among pebbles along the shoals of life.
Before us in saintly array are the Religious Heads —
 true alchemists in the spiritual art,
Competent to treat the ills of the soul, and the dust
 of Whose Feet works as a potent charm.

We are here to welcome the Beloved Master Who
  makes manifest the Holy Light in men;
He holds the panacea for all ills and His shadow is
  a benediction divine.
Everyone, whatever the measure, gets from Him
  something of the glory of God.
The people of the East and the West share alike His
  vintage of love and partake in the feast divine.

Thou hast striven hard to bring the Kingdom of God
  down to the lowly earth;
Thou hast awakened all to the verities of life by
  giving glory and greatness to the soul,
And like Sawan-rain, poured Thy bounties on the
  burning sands of time,
And like a Divine Godman on the God-way, hath
  come to ferry the floundering souls in Lethe.

Thou hast made manifest in man, the saving
  life-line of Holy Light and Sacred Sound;
Thou hast led the long-parted lovelorn soul back to
  her bridal bed in heaven above;
Thy celestial Light hath enriched the earth a
  thousand-fold, and raised the glory of ancient
  India.
O! Grant us but a drop from Thy tankard divine,
  and allow us to kiss the dust of Thy Feet!

Let us all join hands in Thy Holy Cause—to
  transform the prevailing gloom into a rosy dawn!
Let us awaken the thirst for spiritual experience,
  the crowning glory of human birth!
Let us share alike the joys and sorrows of the world,
  shedding freely the light of peace and amity!
Let us like radii converge at one center, meet in
  one God—the live center of all!

THE CRY OF THE SOUL

The Third Conference of World Religions, of which Sant Kirpal Singh Ji was the President, was held in Delhi in 1965. It was for that occasion that this poem was composed and recited.

Listen Ye to the piteous cry of the soul
Writhing in agony and wailing for union with Thee.

Pain and pestilence are prevailing,
And clouds of distress have dampened the spirit of Man.

The rushing gales are putting out the lamp
That hitherto lighted man's path in the dark.

The world is engaged in reaching the planets,
But no one discovers a balm that soothes.

No one shares the misery of the other man,
None to heal the human heart.

The powerful atom has bewitched the world,
But the soul has lost its halo, its glory.

The earth is afire with the cold flame of war;
Rubble and rot descend from every side.

The spirit of Man is shrivelling in a deadly grip of steel,
And is reduced to a bundle of cracking bones.

On Thee, O Gracious God, the world casts its eyes;
Save it from extinction at this critical hour.

Let unity and love prevail on all planes of creation,
And Thy chosen Messengers preach the love divine.

It is love that enraptures all hearts wherever they
   may be,
As fragrance exudes from the flowers in all gardens.

All peoples of this earth weigh equal,
Heading as they are toward one goal, common to
   all.

It is one Master Who serves the vintage to all:
All eyes gain Light from Him.

All rivers spring from one common fount,
But look as different as surging, struggling waves.

So we being nurslings of the same mother earth,
Owe allegiance to the divine Father above.

We are His scions, and He is our Lord,
He is the Lord of all, and we worship Him, and Him
   alone.

Tipplers of the same divine wine, let us be knit
   in love;
Our colorful exteriors vary but we are one in heart.

All firestones, despite their different shapes, strike
   the same fire;
All cows—white, brown, black or brindle—give
   the same white milk.

Everyone holds a different measure in his hand,
But is equal in the tavern of life.

Let all come forth and march in loving union;
The greater the trials, the more united we shall be.

Together we shall overpower the onslaught of time,
And learn to light the torch of love in one and all.

Let us all unite in the name of God,
And save mankind from spiritual fall.

Let us find the remedy which raises us from the
   wheel of life,
Fills our whole being with love, and alchemizes us
   into the divine.

This hope of union kindles our hearts,
But we know not the way.

O God, lead us aright; give us courage,
Help us to live up to the Great Masters' ideals.

Unite us in a love which surges into our life-stream,
Making our lives a symphony, soft and sweet.

The soul cries for the dawn that smiles at the weary
   wayfarer,
And for the divine Light to embrace the whole
   cosmos.

MASTER OF LIGHT AND LIFE

This poem was written in honor of Sant Kirpal Singh Ji in the 1960's.

O Friend of humanity, Thou leadeth the way to peace.
O Light of the world, Thou Lighteth every soul.
Thou hath filled everyone with the love of God,
And their faces shine forth with the glory divine.

All the lovers of God get their wisdom from Thee,
The body and the soul both live in harmony through Thee.
The world looks up to Thee for showers of bliss,
As Thou bringeth comforting peace to lacerated hearts.

Now that the world has withered to the very roots,
And people are beset with delusion and distress,
Thou hath brought down a message of hope from God above,
A message that is common for the Family of Man.

Thou doth come upon the earth in different times and climes,
And yet showereth Thy life-giving rain equally on all.
The distress of the world-weary shakes Thee to Thy very depth,
And Thou hasteneth, attired in the human garb, to suffer our woes.

In Thy august presence all sins fly like autumn leaves,
And heaven's peace descends on earth from end to end.

Thou art a panacea for all the ills that afflict the soul,
And the darkness of ignorance shunneth Thee from afar.

May we live eternally under the shadow of Thy holy wings,
And may Thy glorious reign continue forever!
May Thy glance of grace be on us day and night,
And may we ever have our fill of the elixir divine!

Engaged in the service of man, Thou art ever on the move,
For Thou can'st not stand unconcerned at human woes.
The oneness of life is the quintessence of Thy teachings,
And Thou uniteth human beings in bonds of love.

The Universe with all its forms and colors is but one;
Thou art a manifestation of the Unmanifest.
A veritable knower of all about the house of God;
Thou art an endless ocean of love and bestower of eternal life.

Thou hath brought the Kingdom of God on earth,
And initiated us into the secrets of the Beyond.
Thou art gifted with the divine attributes of Sawan,
And Thou maketh visible the invisible workings of God.

All Thy creatures are intoxicated with the love divine,
And the soul steeped in that love is freed from all toil.

Showereth Thou happiness on the peoples of the earth,
And the lamps of Thy love shine in all their shrines.

Thou art Word-made-flesh, and love is Thy only creed,
Thy message is the message of ages that India preached.
God hath sent Thee to make His Will manifest in man,
And to free man from the fear of death.

Thou leadeth mankind to the kindly Celestial Light,
And the world adores Thee as an Authority from above.
All Thy tipplers sing paeans to Thee, Beloved Master,
May Thou continue blessing them through Thy God-intoxicated eyes!

Thy elixir of life transmutes this dross life,
And harmonizes man, making an angel of him.
May Thy mercy pour forth on all who come unto Thee!
May the thirsty quench their thirst with the Water of Life!

May we drink freely from Thy soul-enlivening eyes,
And may we carry Thy message of Love far and wide!
May our soulful prayers rise to the heavens above,
So that Thou liveth eternally, ever guiding man to God!

O God! Let the Light of Thy mercy envelop our
   tavern,
And let the divine vintage of Kirpal flow forever!

FELICITATIONS

On the occasion of the Diamond Jubilee Celebrations for Sant Kirpal Singh Ji which were held on 6th February 1969 in Delhi, this poem was recited.

Let us lift our hands in thanksgiving unto the Lord,
For the Keeper of His tavern is so lavish with
  vintage divine,
And whosoever tastes of it gets apparelled in
  celestial Light;
The gates of heaven are opened unto him and he
  dances in ecstasy.

The entire creation is aglow with the Light of Thy
  Life,
And the Holy Light from Thee is elevating and
  ennobling;
It brings with it the perfume of love from the garden
  of the Lord.
O! wait a while, and enjoy a whiff of the heavenly
  breeze.

Thy emblazoned sign hath cast a spell around the
  tavern,
And all seem irresistibly drawn to Thee from far
  and near.
"Be good, do good, be one" is Thy soul-stirring
  message to the world;
It hath inspired the Family of Man to take the path
  of unity.

This is Thy rich dower coming to Thee from Sawan
  the Munificent,

And this He brought to Thee from the beginning of time,
So that it could survive through Thee till the end of time,
And man, blessed with Knowledge Divine, may live happily forever.

It is through Thy grace that human hearts blossom forth,
And commingle their fragrance in the vast sea of life.
Thou makest men fear-free from the afflictions of the earth,
And in Thy spiritual aura they live enjoying perfect peace and harmony.

All humankind hold Thee in loving reverence sweet,
And are ready to sacrifice themselves at the altar of Thy love.
May Thy ensign remain ever aloft and above the din of the world,
And may we have occasions evermore to celebrate Thy advent on earth!

May Thou heartily live amongst us till the end of the world,
And may we through Thee have a fill of bliss unto the last,
Eternally singing of Thee and of Thy message of love to Man,
And coming to Thy Lotus Feet athirst for the nectar of love!

May Thou cleanse us of the multitude of our sins,
And initiate us into the secrets of life forever!
May the deluded world become a haven of everlasting bliss,
And the kingdom of Heaven be established on this earth!

Let the earth bloom with roses fresh and sweet,
And heaven's Light shine in every human heart!
May Thy charged words impart bliss to every restless soul,
And the strains of Thy song of peace envelop the dreary world!

Let all mankind be knit in the silken bonds of love,
And let all live in the sunshine of Thy glory!
Let all faiths, beliefs and creeds find a solace in Thee,
And man be happy as man no matter what they be!

May the shadow of Thy protecting wings remain ever on the earth,
And may this tavern of Thine flourish more and more!
May Thou ingrain in us the essence of love and peace,
And bestow on us the heavenly bliss which knows no end!

CHAMPION OF THE CARAVAN OF LOVE
(Mahatma Gandhi)

This poem was written in 1969 to commemorate the Centenary of Mahatma Gandhi's birth, and was recited on the All India Radio.

Friends, the frail exterior,
And the weakness of limbs—
Why bemoan?
For soul is the conqueror of the cosmos.
Whenever the force of materialism
Strikes against the power of spirituality,
The former crumbles like a house built on sand.

A skeleton of bones, a handful of clay,
Whom the hard granite walls couldn't deter;
A magic touch of his hand
Turned pointed bayonets into sheaves of corn.
Does the sun accept defeat from the dark night?

You are the Soul of the tormented souls of the earth,
Of the starved and naked millions,
Of the wailing, helpless folk,
Of the widow's mate caught up in the flames of war—
The war waged for independence.
Might failed to smash that powerful soul
As strong rock fails to smother a tender sapling.

A warrior who stakes his all in the great struggle
Scorns to die on a comfortable bed.
He gulps the cup of death when the call comes
And exposes his proud chest to the death-dealing bullets.

You are a votary of non-violence,
A champion of the caravan of love!
Your blood gave tint to the soil;
Like oil it will be poured into more and more
    lamps—
Illuminating and showing the path,
As the caravan moves on.

THE ELIXIR OF LOVE

This poem was written for and recited at the Fourth Conference of World Religions held in Delhi in 1970.

How is it that man is torn away from man,
And love, the cementing force, is all out of gear?

How is it that we hear the clash of arms all around,
And the blood in man is on fire with lust and greed?

How is it that Peace and Truth have disappeared from the earth,
And the flowers have lost all their fragrant bloom,
And the life of man on earth has become a veritable hell?

Alas! man is playing in the hands of his own inventions,
And science has opened unto him the flood of energy pent in matter.
He is out to conquer Venus, Jupiter and the Moon,
And dreams of rising to the heavenly heights of the Sun.

Armed with the might of atom, he grows and waxes strong,
And the flight of the soul is just a flickering shadow on the wall.

Tossing on the high tide of pelf, power and plenty,
He revels in his animal strength, delighting in the pleasure of the senses,
And is mightily engaged in cutting at the very roots of his life.

Let these silvery shadows pass from the earth,
And let us build a new world with new hopes and new desires;
Let us cultivate love in the hearts of men,
And let all tread the Path of Love—
The Path shown, time and again, by the spiritually great,
The Path sanctified by the great Master Sawan,
The Path illumined by the Light of Kirpal,
So that we all travel happily together like members of one caravan,
And live in peace—the inward peace of the soul,
And move moth-like towards the Father of lights,
With love-laden eyes intoxicated with Love Divine,
Love surging in and out from the very pores of the body.
Let all the tipplers dance merrily with cups full of inebriating wine—
Whether in the Diwans of Delhi or in the Persian palaces.

Let all human differences sink, sink never to rise again,
And the earth wear once again a floral look as on a festal day,
And the world be free from fears of storm and stress,
And men live in constant joy, with the love of God in their hearts,
And then we may have a heaven on earth for which we so vehemently pray.

IN MEMORIAM

This tribute was paid at Sawan Ashram, Delhi, on 13th April 1970, in sweet memory of the poet's mother who had merged with the Oversoul on 3rd April 1970.

Dear Mother, my heart is heavy and sad
On your eternal physical parting;
The apparel of love is torn asunder.
With the benevolence of Lord Sawan,
You were an apostle of human kindness.
The companionship of the Master
Made you an ideal and pious being.
You were an ideal life partner, a kind mother,
An embodiment of Truth, Piety and Spirituality.

You brought me up in the lap of affection,
And imbued me with wisdom and culture.
Your sweet words taught me social manners,
Gave a glow to my mind,
And sharpness to my intellect.
The spirit of love I gained from your sweet nature,
And my heart learnt the art of loving humanity.
"Love is the panacea of all ills"—
You taught me this golden principle,
In fact you blessed your small child with the wisdom
    of life.
Woe betide me! I am now bereft of your affection,
Your elevating glimpses, your ennobling radiance.

You were a symbol of service and sacrifice;
When the world was sad,
You shared its deep sadness.
You were humble and kind
To all your kith and kin,

Lived according to the will of the Master,
And served selflessly the poor, the afflicted.
You sacrificed all your comforts and possessions
For the sake of faith,
For the service of multitudes.
You had no greed for pelf,
And lived for serving the Master.
Though your exterior grew weak day by day,
Yet your spirit remained indomitable,
For the mystic flame within you was ever young and
 strong.

A smile bloomed on your lips;
You closed your eyes and were one with your
 Master.
The beam got absorbed in the sun, and you became
 one with the Word.
Contented were you in heart and soul,
With the mysteries of the world now all revealed,
The light merged in the Light.
As your spirit winged its way heavenward,
And you stood face to face with the Lord,
You left the body cheerfully,
And attained salvation by the Grace of God.
The Master bade you farewell with a smile,
As He had done to His father, mother and brothers.
You bequeathed a message to the world:
"It is the love of humanity
 that earns immortality."

You have passed through this mortal world
As fragrance passes through the valley of death.
Your sweet character, your noble behavior,
Taught us how to love every living creature;

Death has only opened a new chapter in your life.
To the enlightened, you are life eternal.
The cool soft heavenly breeze
Is blowing for you in your Abode Eternal.
Though you are no longer physically with us,
Yet the silent voice of your affection still remains,
And your blessings showered upon us will last
    forever.

THE EMBODIMENT OF LOVE DIVINE

This poem in four parts was written to celebrate the Beloved Master's return to India after His Third World Tour, and was recited in Delhi on 6th February 1973.

What a blessed day for the tipplers of the tavern
When the divine Cup-Bearer manifested Himself.

With a heart overflowing with kindness
He has come in flesh to share our woes.

At His clarion call the world-weary form into a caravan,
And He leads the caravan to its destined end.

He has taught mankind the lesson of Universal Love,
As He holds a Commission to weld them into one.

His divine effulgence has filled the world,
And in our midst He shines like the Sun.

His apron is full of flowers of various hues,
And He, a veritable gardener in the garden of the earth.

The Sun of Spirituality has risen above
To awaken the souls from their deep slumber.

§ § § § §

Welcome are to Thee the spiritual gatherings—
Gatherings grown great in decades two and a half.

In memory of Thy Master Thou hast set up an Ashram
Where the Light of Love and Truth shines day and night.

Thrice hast Thou gone round the world on a Mission of Peace
With the miraculous torch of Thy Master to shed lustre abroad.

By Thy precept and practice Thou hast enlivened the West—
The West plunged head-over-heels in material realms.

Thou hast revealed to them the goal of life,
And unravelled for them the mystery of death.

Thou hast once again revived the ancient glory of India,
And restless hearts have found peace at Thy Feet.

Thou hast knit human souls with the Oversoul,
And the world has grown richer by Thy spiritual wealth.

§ § § §

Fortunate are we, O comrades all
To have the Cup-Bearer once again in our midst.

He hath broadcast the Message of Love and Peace,
He, the Friend of all and the True Guide on the Way.

Having lit the Light of God in all human hearts,
He has returned to His fold in the East.

His Message is one of Unity, Friendship and Goodwill;
For Him all mankind is but a family of God.

All beings, wheresoever, are pearls scattered far and wide,
Like so many beads on the string of Love.

All differences of caste, color and creed become dust and ashes
When the Fire-of-God is lit in the human heart.

He laid the foundation of Manav Kendra, a Center for service to man and land;
It is a veritable home for the aged, lost and forlorn to live in peace.

Here man shall learn to rise above body and mind,
And shall be free from all sorrows and sufferings.

Here spirituality shall thrive by leaps and bounds,
And the Light of God shall fill the space around.

§ § § §

All friends and comrades joined together this day
Pray that the Living Light of Life may shine forever.

May He resolve for us all the mysteries of life and death,
And keep the garden of the earth in full bloom.

May the young saplings under His charge grow in
    stature sublime,
And His protective Hands keep all free from harm.

May the world resound with His Heavenly Melodies,
And its people grow in peace, power and plenty.

May this Embodiment of Love continue to guide
    mankind,
And all evil influences disappear from this earth.

May the forces of darkness melt into the blazing
    Light of God,
And His Light keep the lustre lit for all time to
    come.

May this Divine Tavern attract people from far and
    near,
And its Light enlighten the eyes of all.

ADVENT OF THE UNIVERSAL CUP-BEARER

This poem was recited on 6th February 1974, during the First Unity of Man Conference held in Delhi.

As the fragrant zephyr bloweth, so doth flow the vintage divine, for there hath come the harbinger of spring;
With the wave of a hand from the Beloved Cup-Bearer, the tavern is humming with life and the cup is ever on the move.

Let the tipplers of the world rejoice for Thou hast ushered in a perpetual spring with colorful wine without measure;
I would fain sacrifice myself for I have learnt Thy message of love—the message having borne fruit in abundance.

Thou, a veritable guide on the way to Truth, the Light of God and soul of faith, hast spread far and wide the message of Sawan.
Thy celestial abode is so high that even the moon and the sun reverently turn round to pay obeisance at Thy door.

When once the bird of the spirit is caught in Thy love, it becomes forever free from the ties of mind and matter.
On the Path of Love there doth come a stage when the devotees of their own accord fall on their faces before Thee.

Whenever the wayfarers of life are engulfed in the storm and stress of the world, Thy name invariably comes to their lips.
Thy message of true love and infinite mercy girdling the globe, testifies Thy divine plan to salvage mankind.

O munificent God, praise be unto Thee, for Thou hast sent a kindly confessor to the defaulters on earth;
And all the places of worship are, this day, clothed in holy joy, for each one hath found the benevolent saviour.

Let the happy tidings go forth to all thirsty souls far and wide;
The Beloved of the Universe hath come, and they can drink freely from His soul-enlivening eyes.

O Darshan, the heavenly glory has descended on this earth in Kirpal to illuminate the East as well as the West.

ELEGY ON THE PASSING AWAY OF THE BELOVED MASTER

This was recited at Sawan Ashram, Delhi, on 1st September 1974, at the Bhog Ceremony for Sant Satguru Kirpal Singh Ji Maharaj.

He who was human to the core has gone.
He who served the vintage divine has gone.
He who strove for peace in the world has gone.
>With His passing darkness stalks abroad,
>And earth is mantled in sable shrouds.

Who is there to light the flame of life?
Who is there to justify ways of God to man?
Who is there to soothe our lacerated hearts?
>Our Best Beloved has gone from our midst.
>Alas! He has left us to mourn His loss.

He was the uncrowned King of human hearts,
He sang nectarean melodies from the Granth and the Quran.
O! How sweetly love flowed from His eyes!
>The lute of the Gita and the Gospel is mute,
>The lamp is shattered and the light has gone.

All distinctions of castes and creeds are made by man,
All divisions of lands and nations separate man from man.
He brought harmony amidst divisions.
>Unity in diversity being His answer to all ills,
>To share in the griefs of others was His Creed.

We have lost a sure guide and an unfailing friend,
A friend who in the darkness of the soul enkindled
   Light.
But why mourn this physical parting?
>   Death has no sway over the Elect;
>   Sages like Him know not death.

In trials and tribulations They are ever by our side,
And pilot us to the destined end.
How can death stop Them from Their work?
>   He is alive, more alive than ever before;
>   Why mourn Him who knows no death?

He may have gone from our physical sight,
Yet in reality He is ever with us,
And is ever present right in our midst,
>   Giving out His oft repeated Message,
>   The Message of One God, One Man and One
>   World.

He still sings to us the Song of the Soul,
He still pours out the quintessence of Love,
He is ever leading Souls onward to God.
>   He left the world in all His glory,
>   Leaving us in tears to mourn the loss.

Throughout His life He knew no rest;
At home and abroad He was ever at work,
Enkindling God's Love in human breasts.
>   How can the glory of Sawan fade?
>   How can the Mission of Kirpal fail?

Let us pledge to dedicate our lives to Him,
And for the work for which He came,
We bow unto Him—the Lord of the Tavern;
    May His Message spread far and wide!
    May the dignity of man ever rise high!

Let us be true to His paeans of love,
Let us be true to the memory of Kirpal,
Let us walk abreast in His footsteps.
    Let us be good and engage in goodly deeds,
    Let all mankind be knit together in peace.

BOOKS AND LITERATURE ON THE TEACHINGS OF THE MASTERS

By Kirpal Singh

A Brief Life Sketch of Baba Sawan Singh Ji Maharaj
Man, Know Thyself
The Jap Ji: The Message of Guru Nanak
Ruhani Satsang: Science of Spirituality
Baba Jaimal Singh: His Life & Teachings
Prayer: Its Nature & Technique
Spirituality: What It Is
Naam or Word
Simran: The Sweet Remembrance of God
The Crown of Life: A Study in Yoga
Seven Paths to Perfection
Morning Talks
The Teachings of Kirpal Singh (edited by Ruth Seader):
Vol. I: The Holy Path
Vol. II: Self-Introspection/Meditation
Vol. III: The New Life
Heart to Heart Talks: Vols. I & II (edited by Malcolm Tillis)
The Wheel of Life: The Law of Action & Reaction
God Power, Christ Power, Master Power
Godman
Spiritual Elixir
The Mystery of Death
How to Develop Receptivity

By Other Authors

The Saint and His Master, by B.M. Sahai
and Radha Krishna Khanna
The Beloved Master, by Bhadra Sena
Ocean of Grace Divine, edited by Bhadra Sena

SAT SANDESH is a monthly magazine devoted to the teachings of Hazur Baba Sawan Singh Ji, Param Sant Kirpal Singh Ji, and the living Master Sant Darshan Singh Ji. It features discourses, poetry, photographs and illustrated reports of the Master's activities, etc. Write Sat Sandesh, 8528 Evesham Road, Richmond, Virginia 23229, U.S.A.

INFORMATION AND LITERATURE AVAILABLE FROM THE FOLLOWING CENTERS:

THE UNITED STATES

Mr. T.S. Khanna
General Representative
8807 Lea Lane
Alexandria, Virginia 22309

Olga Donenberg
6007 N. Sheridan Rd. #14-B
Chicago, Illinois 60660

Sunnie Cowen
3976 Belle Vista Dr. E.
St. Petersburg Beach, Florida 33706

Sawan Kirpal Meditation Center
Rt. 1, Box 24
Bowling Green, Virginia 22427

Ruth Seader
8 Copper Beech Pl.
Merrick, New York 11566

Bruno Zaffina
P.O. Box 11385
Ft. Lauderdale, Florida 33339

Mary Skene
1568 S. Genesee Ave.
Los Angeles, California 90019

Michael Grayson
8528 Evesham Rd.
Richmond, Virginia 23229

CANADA

Dr. Roger Foisy
9531 De Chateaubriand Ave.
Montreal, H2M1Y3, Quebec

Juaneva Smith
General Delivery
Quathiaski Cove
British Columbia

MEXICO	Carmen Uribe Vargas Artega 10-12 Cuernavaca, Morelos
SOUTH AMERICA	J. Ricardo Nunez Apdo. Aereo 4485 Carrera 6a No. 15-85 Cali, Colombia
	Carlos A. Lozano Apdo. Aereo 6847 Cali, Colombia
	Jorge Leon Ferro Apdo. Aereo 2092 Cali, Colombia
	Carlos Maldonado Galvis Carrera 56-A No. 8-72 Bogota 6, Colombia
	Maria Antonia De Vargas Calle 8A No. I-45 El Prado Popayan, Colombia
	Juan G. Torres Apdo. Aereo 82 Medellin, Colombia
	L.A. Rajkumar 6E Ramphal St. Hampshire Corentyne, Berbice Guyana
	Ranold Ramroop 97B Laluni St., Queenstown Georgetown, Guyana
	Ernesto Valladares P.O. Box 394 Quito, Ecuador

ENGLAND	Mr. B.R. Misra 11 Leander Rd. (Off Kensington Rd.) Northolt, Middlesex UB5 6TE
	Geraldine Horton Dittons Corner Pevensy Rd. Polegate, Sussex BN266HR
GERMANY	Hilde Dressel Gustav Warnerstrasse 19 729 Freudenstadt, West Germany
	Brigitte Boehm Heimstrasse 8 7015 Korntal, West Germany
FRANCE	Betta Mouangue Joseph 3 Square du Nouveau Belleville 75020 Paris
SWITZERLAND	Mrs. Angela Seiler Lenggstrasse 24 8008 Zurich
AFRICA	Anyi Agwudagwu P.O. Box 20 Ogwashi-Uku, Nigeria
	Yao Assare, Attorney P.O. Box 3789 Accra, Ghana
	Hon. K. Azina Nartey, Jr. Judges' Chambers Circuit Court P.O. Box 153, Sunyani Ghana, West Africa

	Mathias E. Inegbaligha Produce Inspection Division P.M.B. 5011 Port Harcourt, Rivers State Nigeria, West Africa
AUSTRALIA	Leslie Dosa 7/25 Melton St. Somerton Pk. 5044 South Australia
MAURITIUS	Dr. Meeranaidoo T. Somanah 20 Icery St. Forest Side Mauritius, (Indian Ocean)
INDONESIA	Eddie Boon Hotel Kebayoran Inn Jalan Senayan 87 Kebayoran Baru, Jakarta Selatan

The Living Master Sant Darshan Singh Ji Maharaj resides at 219 Laxmibai Nagar, New Delhi, India 110023.